gutter flowers

Don Welch

Gutter Flowers

By Don Welch

Cover design and layout by Edmund Elfers
All photographs by Jim Reese

ISBN: 0-9674123-8-2

Logan House
Route 1 Box 154
Winside, Nebraska 68790

www.LoganHousePress.com

"Books Are Heavy"

Table of Contents

I

II

III

IV

Foreword

Don Welch, in "Alley Poet"—one of many strikingly terse poems in this collection—says it best: "he's learned to read / the taste of smells." Yes, and I'd add with a minimum of words he evokes a maximum of feelings and sympathies. One superb example is "For the Battered Girl Who Always Said Hello." At the end of the poem, having heard the girl's attempt to say hello—that "fuse of orange traveling from (her) tongue"—he calls her "a lily in that alley. / One." In the Sunday school I attended, long ago, we sang of Christ being "the lily of the valley, the bright and morning star." My guess is that Don Welch knows that song, and knows also that holiness can reveal itself in more ways than one. That battered girl, with her hello, is the living embodiment of kindness's occasional victory over persecution, and Welch is the living embodiment of a poet who has the sensibility to acknowledge it and the skills to record it.

There are other figures in the alley, of course—the man whose yard is a garden, "his eyes growing squash" as he stands on his porch anticipating another season; the old Slovak woman whose "hose flap like loose flesh / in the wind" as she wields a hoe; the elderly man at the edge of town who works to erect a wire fence, "to have it right," as he puts it, and Welch appreciates considerably the old man's honesty no less than his dedication: "This morning, in the pewter light, / he has the scars to prove it"; and his "lady of the alley," a woman of indeterminate age who rummages through garbage looking for aluminum cans, which she offers to the poet, who I believe declines, but who does not miss the sacred overtones of the moment: "My lady of the alley, / toothless, / full of alms."

Welch moves among the poor like a modern day Whitman who has mastered the fine art of pruning. The poor, he says, "need the dump and truck of love / to walk on too." And the rest of us need the poet's words to bring us those places we have neither the time nor the courage to explore. "In a world gone wrong," he writes in "Early Morning Song," "sing a counter-song." In this poem, and in others, he does the singing for us, reminding us that, even in gutters, flowers bloom: "In the cracks of the curbs, / among the butts and condoms, they are the future / chaliced in the present..." Chaliced. That's the touch. And Don Welch knows how to touch.

William Kloefkorn
Nebraska State Poet

~for Art Pierce,
word-worker

I

Alleys

Where the doors are off,
and there's an air which says, "Come in."

Where the only way's toward the other end,
and ruts of meaning last as long as frost.

Where griefs, like rocks, are found in beds.

To the left, chained dogs.
To the right, a mess of kittens.

Where rust is crippling every nail,
where odors, crashing, lose their fenders.

Where nothing's lost, and everything's tossed in.

Narrow islands, the ends of which are clear.

Advent

This morning
two new parents have pulled up
in a driveway of mud,

the driver's door
with its pane of cellophane
swinging open,

the driver himself
slouching toward the house,
a cigarette in his mouth,

while the woman,
kicking open her door,
carries in a single green blanket

something unseen. Hurt, cut,
she takes each step a foot at a time.
The air is already lonely.

After the Abuse

Like fog
something is always mothering
the willows

and on the nerve ends
of the locusts
growing pure tears.

The Young Widow

The young widow has planted
moss rose in the drainage
of her cesspool at the farthest
reaches of her house.

Obscured by the pig weed,
it is rarely seen, so low
it goes unnoticed even
by the bees. Why, then,

using a corn knife,
would she cut a path next
to the seepage to look upon
the flowers whose centers bleed?

Consider God, apparently
like this in His needs.

Don Welch

For the Boy Who Told Me Men Don't Cry

How can I show you
the tear in the world's eye,

that pure fault,
that cold scald,

that bead which is
a lead necklace;

that mirror in which
all our sorrows appear,

that ash so clear
it is cinderless?

Behind the Monument Company

An angel, one wing gone,
lies on its side.

There are no pupils
in its eyes.

What it's always stood for
is dead reckoning.

This morning a cat,
curled up on the stump

of the angel's wing,
is making a warm poultice in the sun.

Above them are windows
plaqued with dust.

The cat soothes the angel
with no fuss.

Labor Day

— among meatpacking boners and cutters

All day a good wind
has been washing their houses.

All day it's been a soft brush
on their crucified bodies,
their invisible shadow.

For hours it's played every sound legato,
it's passed like light through
the glass.

They've never asked,
"Show us the palm of your presence"
or "Rub us with the souls of soft stars."

Only now,
at the end of the evening,
has it turned their wounds into scars.

Flowering Plum Bush

This is the way the snow should smell,
handfuls of aromas on black spines.

This afternoon a bush of deep conviction sings.
Spring is turning winter inside out.

Look: on the branches' long arthritic fingers
there are the petals of soft shouts.

While Leaning against a Garbage Can
behind the Prince of Peace Church

It is Tuesday.
The ordinary kingdom has come.
Again the usual is spiritual.

So I pick a number.
Like One.

One garbage man walking along.
A bush green with the sun.
A church and its shadow in love.

And leaning against a garbage can,
I keep looking at One,
going in through its intricate oval,
finding it more than its sum.

Early Morning Walk

So when does an odyssey begin?

From what morning whose step?
From what egg in the air
the ghost of which foot?

And in the distance what lure-bird is calling?

So go on.
Step off with nothing in your hand.
Believe that rhythms are a visionary sense.

In a world gone wrong, sing a counter-song.
The unsayable yearns to be said.

Remembering Slobodan Milosevich

The old man's pigeons are called Swing Pouters,
their bodies saddled with red wings,
their chests inflated like small globes.

Flying up, their wings like pistol shots
throughout his neighborhood,
they applaud the old man's world.

Their origin: old Balkan birds,
blue Slavic skies, where children,
raped and clubbed, turned maggot-eyed.

Old Polish Woman

Every morning she brings the light to facts,
asking it in, sitting it down, offering
her brown hands.

Taking from her cupboard a plate on which
nothing has occurred, she imagines
for the light a word.

But nothing like the darkness of decay
which fell upon bombed bodies,
nor the hellish flares

which burned their insides out.
Here, take, eat, she says,
and the light,

which has just come from the fermentation
of sweet reason, begins smelling
like fresh bread.

My Lady of the Alley

Sagging,
she struggles from her back door
to the alley,
her flesh hanging upon her
like a girdle,
the stays of which
are lost.

"Need aluminum cans?"
she asks.

I smile,
watching her
go through her garbage
with scarred palms.

My lady of the alley,
toothless,
full of alms.

The Greeting of a Hispanic Man Lying in a Hammock on a Cold Day

"Hey."

Alley Poet

Like an old dog
pulling a hamburger wrapper
through a fence,
he's learned to read
the taste of smells.

Gutter Flowers

II

Gutter Flowers

South Side Greeting

The retarded man waves from his porch,
the flesh under his biceps a happy flag
helloing the world.

"Hey, you," he yells,
his sweat pants pulled up until
his crotch is just under his armpits.

"Great day," I sing back,
my Red Wing boots on fire with the sun.
"Goodbye," he replies, his hand up over his head

like a fine Spanish dancer.
And I remember his greeting clear through
the avenues clogged with exhaust,

long after it should be lost
in the town's combustible seriousness.

South Side Dogs

Approaching a backyard where a travel van
is up on blocks, its windows smashed;

where the smell of a chicken coop is green,
and its fence coarse enough to let things in,

not out, you'll be greeted by two dogs,
a bouncer and a maitre d'.

The one with the quicker yip will be Spitz;
the other huge and pure mongrelian.

Then, from beneath the porch, their children
will scurry out, little waiters in the sun,

the snubs of love. Through the gate
they'll lift their legs and pee.

On the Playground

The whites have turned their backs on the black,
their heads cocked over their shoulders,
their lips pulled back, their mouths open,

full of yellow teeth. It's recess,
and as the dominant male twirls a football
in his hand and laughs, two girls

with golden manes break into smiles.
Hate's a look, a feint, a stench.
The teacher on the playground does her nails.

Pickup Game in the Park

In the late afternoon a lefty pitches the ball
five feet outside the plate,

and the outfielders let go
with a cacophony of profanity.

As he pitches again, the ball right over,
the batter swinging two feet above the ball,

the outfielders turn their fingers
into adult obscene.

It's baseball time for seven-year-olds,
where hours are supposed to be minutes,

but are really days,
and everyone's frozen into position.

As the pitcher kicks a wound into the mound
and the catcher becomes a crab behind the plate,

an outfielder chases a butterfly
toward a fence which says OPTIMIST.

It's August, and the game is running late.

Hard Kids

Get under the dirt
on their faces
and you'll find
wounds almost
scarred shut,
or mouths
from which joys
occasionally
bleed out.

Right now
it's midnight,
and they're riding
their bikes down
the slides
in the park,
metal knifing metal,
incisions
in the dark.

Newer Testament Stuff

"Get your ass back here,"
the fat man working under
the hood of his Sunbird
shouts at his son, the boy

flipping off his old man
with his finger. "That's
my beer," the old man yells,
the boy, cocking his arm,

threatening to send the bottle
back at his old man's head.
Never were the hops
of the fields harvested

with less biblical dread,
the son, dropping his drawers,
mooning his father, while
waddling spiritually ahead.

Running Off

"Come back,
you little shit,"
she says,

      her words
like a broken bottle
aimed at the back
of his head.

Like Poverty

Like poverty
you always knew
she would come,

dog crap fouling
her dress, cat hair
wrapped around

the strings of her shoes,
her bruises, black
iron peonies.

You always knew
she'd walk all the way
across town

to stand on
your porch as
a perversion of blue,

her finger hooked
in her mouth,
her nose leaking snot,

her eyes like
the heads
of cold screws.

Welfare Visit

If the boy with no conscience
sets fire to a cat in his own backyard
or body slams his younger brother
across a picnic table still warm

from original recipe or extra crispy,
who's going to look through the windows
of his house and tell you no one's home?
And if they entered, and moved through

vacant rooms, finding no feces on the walls,
no urine stains or bloody belts or canes,
which one of them, emerging from the house,

could tell you that within this place
light lurks, or that in the closet of this kid
cunning breeds with smirks?

With Faded Eyes and a Dirty Dress

Wasn't she too made
to throw her smiles
like boomerangs into
a come-back world,

to watch them arc
through an air as rightly
fair, as sound as any
love has wrought?

Wasn't she too made
to be light's giggles
in the trees, a salt
of sorts to congregations

of dark sentences?
What is there about
the wrong which sacks
a girl like this,

that leaves her standing
in an alley with faded eyes,
a dirty dress, her cheeks
a bruised redundance;

smelling for all the world
like hope gone wrong,
and ordered with her sisters
of abundance?

Showing Me Her Dead Dog

The maggots
working through
its coat were pulling
every thread of it
bone tight.

Snarled back,
its lips would be
the last to go,
their loathing
like the nausea
working on
her nose.

Stalled and Empty

A coal train has blocked the crossing
from the poorest part of town,
and as the bug-eyes of the cross-arms
blink a dusty red,
a man in a pickup has gone to sleep,
the bells of the guard-arms
bleating like dull sheep.
The letters of the coal cars
read SF, UP, BN.
"Quit blocking our fucking crossing,"
one of the dirtiest says.

The Quotidian

Like rails
that run
like arteries
over
the backbones
of old ties,
their ballast
loose,
not snug,

what is
the quotidian
if not
the humdrum
of what's done,

the clank
and thwack
of gritty,
bony love?

South Side Recess

A fourth-grade boy has just wrestled down
a girl and taken off her shoes.

Now he is dancing around like a Scot,
as if the shoes in his hands
were the heads of Englishmen, civilized trophies.

The girl, in pink socks, can't get up.
There are too many stickers in her part of the world,
and the boy, now a Pict,
is screaming blue oaths from the top of the swings.

Here comes the Hague,
the teacher from the International Court
of Fourth-grade Tribunals.

Having just cleared the kindergartners,
she's coming on strong,
her flesh holding her back, bouncing around,
and only her mouth is hurrying.

Cinders and Hollyhocks

*"An alley is a dump of bits and pieces
connected by an air of disregard."*

No. An alley's still a poor kid's way to wealth.
No hopes are ever quite so crushed as rocks,
no black-eyed susans unable to seed themselves
in smashed-down fences. It takes the sun,
and an innocent angle of the mind, to make
coal gleam; and the discovery of old hex bolts
can weld minutes into moments. In an alley
no dead cat dies for those who cannot touch it,
no garbage man grows familiar to chained dogs,
and even girls with deep bruises on their cheeks
can twirl hollyhocks between their fingers
and their thumbs, spinning them into rose-hued
ballerinas. In alleys every morning's China,
the chow with the purple tongue.

Don Welch

III

Gutter Flowers

They flower,
and flower for someone
just by flowering.

In the cracks of the curbs,
among the butts and condoms,
they are the future

chaliced in the present,
the case of a mood spun white;
thistle-less in the sun

where heat waves
wave like old Ophelias;
or run.

For the Battered Girl Who Always Said Hello

Emerging from the fist of your house,
you came at me like a sparkler through the weeds,

even in August when the elephant ears
of the rhubarb fainted

and the backbones of old nails
scabbed up in rust.

Near the garbage cans I could count on
a fuse of orange traveling from your tongue.

Like a lily in that alley.
One.

Signs of a Birthday Party

On a broken walk
in the graveled part of town,
there was a form
and name for every guest:

Emma, in purple chalk,
with oval eyes and push-pull hair;
Heather, her eyebrows as thick
as felt erasers;

and Joy, whose lips
performed the perfect ode to space.
And within their universe
of shattered glass

the birthday girl herself
had drawn upon her form new breasts,
two white planets
on a simple A-line dress.

Yet her mouth was as short as fate,
as straight as time.
Only her eyes, two ova,
were a child-like rhyme.

Found Near a Garbage Can

The ripped-off cover of a book,
Bad Girls of the Bible.

On which eyes, like black souls,
were barely veiled.

The part that dark hair plays
in lust almost revealed.

Beside the cover
were three large nails.

Beside the nails,
two stones.

And beyond the fence,
alone,

her skin a lovely covenant
with her bones,

the barest argument
of tones,

lay David's new
Bathsheba.

While Looking Over a Fence
at a Sun-bathing Blonde

Is is sweeter than light.

One glimpse of it
and you talk like a poet.

The Couple

Everything about the man working
on the Ford points crude north,
the way he swears at the wrench,
his fingers too thick to work
the worm gear in its head;
or grinds the starter's teeth,
his anger already running.

And his woman hanging out
the wash, seeing Thursday
through a yellow eye, her lover
having laid one on her?
Needled by despair, the compass
of her heart swings wildly
in search of one magnetic bit.

When in rising from her crate
of sheets she tries to nod,
who will tell her, mostly lying,
that her wash looks good?

Old Couple, Porch Scene

Why isn't the light lingering
in the cathedral of the sun

one hand reaching for another
in the name of love?

Back Porch Scene

The Latino mother's hands fly like doves
across her daughter's confirmation dress,

picking at the ends of its threads,
its pulled-up hem, its raveling life.

Then, stepping back, she holds
in the feathers of her fingers

one small gasp: White Light for Christ,
for Christ White Light,

on the altar of her daughter
onyx-eyed.

An Acre of Butterflies

The Impressionists
never painted
with these yellows.

And couples
never flew with
such light grace.

The blooms
of the alfalfa
are astounded

by the aerial
exclamations
on their page.

Penny Odes

The wag of a half-
blind dog.

Gleams of evening
in the gravel's tongues.

The last acts
of bottle caps.

The mull-less blood.

The gracious pitting
of cement.

The smooth celebrations
of the shade.

The end of a run.

Twilight.

The total sum
of one.

For a New Bride Hanging Out Her Wash

After every song you sing
there is a teal-blue silence,

in which what runs on
is filled with the harmonics of what was.

And when you step beyond
the threshold of your singing,

the air around your shoulders
is a dove's.

Don Welch

On the Antiochian Church

Two pigeons
were making
gullible love;

on a cross
the passion
of two pigeons,

otherwise
orthodox doves.

Alley Pigeon

Torn apart,
one wing was a clutch
of dead fingers

while the other
was a palm
that was lost.

The rest of its life,
now a phantom,
was a clear taking off.

Hard Woman

When she walks through
her backyard, thin as
an alley cat, the weeds
part like a sad breeze.

Her shoulders are as
unleavened as bad yeast,
her breasts cracked and hard
from too much love.

If you were to hold her,
you would note her dirty nose,
her mattered eyes,
the lice which colonize

her ears. And just as
suddenly she'd disappear,
her prints the claw marks
of her years.

Gutter Flowers

Moving

A man with barbed-wire tattoos
has just thrown a mirror
into a pickup's box,
splintering his rage.

With slivered eyes
he's screaming,
"I told you the damn thing
wouldn't fit into the truck,"

while a woman
standing in the hell-hole of their garage
is clinging to a wicker piece
as if it were a child.

Above them
the sparrows coupling in the sun
are taking off for nesting places,
one by one.

IV

The Storefront Doctors

He loves the grids of maps.
She prefers the wind's diagonals.

He loves to know.
She loves to care.

Both hate veneers
and souls that are earnestly off-key.

Neither works with airy thumbs.
Neither is a skimmer of a surface-sort.

Both serve the poor,
and both are tough,

tougher than nails
sucked upon by a thousand mouths of rust.

For the Eight-Year-Old Marked to Be a Poet

They will never christen him.
He has the wrong spots, the wrong tongue,
it doesn't take the dark to make his eyes glow.

Yet growing up among rocks,
he will try to soften their scars,
and wearing the vestments of light,
he will suffer every one of their wars.

At his birth his eyes were blue stars.
Which will collapse when he dies.

At his death they won't say silence swore.

Too Cold

Too cold to snow
the old wives say,
the air too hurt
to cry white tears,
the sky too gray.

Who then brings
us these bouquets
of cold alyssum?
What madness
is reduced to this?

White periods
for the sentences
we cannot write.

Ends, like this,
which fail us
in our failing sight.

One Above

The tree wears the squirrel's nest
like an old corsage,
its leaves hard pressed
by winter.

While along the edges
of the roofs,
icicles hang, gnarled
in their cold descents.

And low, along the sun-line of the snow,
there is a faint crying,
a welling slighter than a tear,
a wintered list, a dying.

Near the Dump

The house with the stained glass windows
used to be a church, its doorways arched,
its cupola a charming vault whose shingles,
rolling up, are lipped with moss.

But set among exotic blues and greens,
a diamond of clear glass is still centered
in each window, as if a clarity
could be surrounded by the gospels.

The walls are dank, the floors a slippery mess,
and to the west, beneath a small rose window,
there's a defaced realtor's sign:
Coldwell-Banker. Call Jesus. Anytime.

Inside Blue's Tavern

Only near the alley door
is the air a snooker green.

Up front, among the ulcerated
stools, it's rot-gut ether.

Shells dust the floor,
conversations lying among them,

and when you step on each,
they sound the same,

as if Blue had taken
the ligaments out of consonants

and eased them into drains.

At Luanne's Speed Wash

A homeless man has just put
four quarters into a speed washer
and is humming an old juke-box song,

> *It's only a paper moon,*
> *sailing over a card-board sea,*
> *but it wouldn't be make-believe*
> *if you believe in me,*

and all two hundred and fifty pounds
of Luanne are dancing,
the gray flesh of her upper arms
like dolphins leaping in a sleeveless sea.

And as the ice in the corners of the windows
slips across the windows' tongues,
the old man, dancing before his Speed Queen,
hums. And hums. And hums.

On a Blistering Day

A gnarled woman in a pickup
is yanking out the skeleton of a hedge,
the osage orange giving up with sucking pops.

Grinding the gears, she's biting the heads
off cigarettes, while engaged in a hard harmony
between the shifter and the shifted.

Flying 30 yards before she brakes,
she gets out, kicks aside the brush,
retrieves her butt, and takes a draw.

Then, hitching up her drawers
and pulling down her bra,
she sets her jaw in tractor low,

while aiming her head-lights
at the block of bark she has to go.

The Man with a Garden for a Yard

The man with a garden for a yard
stands on his porch,
his eyes growing squash,
the air ripe with melons.

It's early March,
but even his terrace has been
plowed and raked,
each clod pulverized by love.

As time winds through his fence,
near the bird bath
new straw bales gleam
like ingots in the sun.

Checking his watch,
he looks out through his screen.
Dirt begins to tendril like a dream.

At the Edge of Town

Hard to know which is more gnarled,
the posts he hammers staples into
or the blue hummocks which run
across his hands like moles.

Work has reduced his wrists
to bones, cut out of him
the easy flesh and brought him
down to this, the crowbar's teeth

caught just behind a barb.
Again this morning
the crowbar's neck will make
its blue slip into wood,

there will be that moment
when too much strength
will cause the wire to break.
But even at 70, he says,

he has to have it right,
and more than right.
This morning, in the pewter light,
he has the scars to prove it.

Old Slovak

In the weeds at the end
of her lot, an old woman
is letting her gnarled fingers
caress her gnarled hoe.

Taking it slow,
she's remembering every rhythm
of pull, bringing herself
up to the handle.

As she's unfolding from herself
the right number of rows,
they're no more, nor less,
than the palpable guess

she's scratched from the years.
Her gray bonnet haloes her face.
Her hose flap like loose flesh
in the wind. In her palm

the pinched lives of the lettuce.
Which she'll drop like
the lives of small angels
into a bed of immaculate rows.

West of Ponticello's Place

Last summer the clover was sweet green,
its yellow blooms big berries
for the bees which went from leaf to leaf,
armored with gold pollen.

Back at their hives, dancing figure-eights,
they mapped their routes, giving
each new worker a sextant from the Queen.
But today the clover's brown.

Heads that glorified the sun
are scabbed like wounds or crowns
slipping from dead helmets.
All around them raw winds swarm.

August Evenings

Evenings, when men who work in packing plants
escape into alleys with long silences
and the crowns of weeds,

where, hanging over fences, they smoke,
the ghosts of their lungs drifting over
the pungent marigolds

and the spent wallets of last year's seeds.
What reconciles any hard place
to itself are its dreams.

Like those evenings, in which
the last light on the gravel gleams.

Among the Poor

Whoever talks philosophy in their alleys
is drunk on the elixir of big words.

Like gravel, what love is
is what love does.

Tough enough to keep weeds down,
hard enough to suffer suns,

it has a look beneath them.
But that's not true.

They need the dump and truck of love
to walk on too.

At the Last Intersection

Walk. Let yourself out again. Be passed on.
A baton for barking dogs. Or silent.
Tickled by foxtail. Fluffed up. Quiet.

Past the shadow of your shadows,
past the hammered world, where
everything's a bent-up love.

Hang true. Be plumb.
Dropping from your crossbeams
through your breast.

If you must intersect with something,
try the sun. Eye level. On the bubble.
Walk. Don't run.